HYMNS

A Portrait Of Christ

HYMNS

A Portrait Of Christ

STEVE GREEN

SPARROW

SPARROW PRESS
NASHVILLE, TENNESSEE

Published 1992 in Nashville, Tennessee, by Sparrow Press,
and distributed in Canada by Christian Marketing Canada, Ltd.

Printed in the United States of America

96 95 94 93 92   5 4 3 2 1

Library of Congress Cataloging-in-Publication Data

Green, Steve.
        Hymns : a portrait of Christ / by Steve Green.
                p.   cm.
        ISBN 0-917143-13-2 (hard cover) : $15.95. — ISBN 0-917143-16-7
(paper) : $8.95
        1. Jesus Christ—Person and offices.   2. Jesus Christ—Devotional
literature.   3. Hymns. English.   I. Title.
        BT205.G65   1992
        245′ .21—dc20   92-28293
                                                           CIP

Design by Barnes & Company

Photo credits: pp. 8-9, 20–21 (inset), 23 (inset), 25 (inset), 34–35—© Rick Browne; pp. 11, 16–17, 22–23, 28–29, 30–31, 34 (inset)—
© David Hazard; pp. 6–7, 8 (inset), 10, 12–13, 14–15, 18, 19, 20–21, 22 (inset), 24–25, 26, 27, 28, 31 (inset), 32–33, 36–37, 38–39—
© Moody Institute of Science

"How Great Thou Art" by Stuart K. Hine
© Copyright 1953 renewed 1981 by MANNA MUSIC, INC., 25510 Avenue Stanford, Suite 101, Valencia, CA 91355.
International copyright secured. All rights reserved. Used by permission.

"Great Is Thy Faithfulness" author: Thomas O. Chisholm, composer: William M. Runyan
© 1923 renewal 1951 by Hope Publishing Company, Carol Stream, IL 60188. All rights reserved. Used by permission.

"Spirit Of The Living God" by Daniel Iverson
© 1935 renewed 1964 by Birdwing Music and BMG Songs, Inc. All rights reserved. International copyright secured.
Used by permission.

"The Lord's Prayer" by Albert Hay Malotte
© 1935 (renewed) G. Shirmer, Inc. All rights reserved. International copyright secured. Used by permission.

Scripture taken from the HOLY BIBLE, NEW INTERNATIONAL VERSION. Copyright
© 1973, 1978, 1984 International Bible Society. Used by permission of Zondervan Bible Publishers.

FOREWORD

How many of us fully appreciate our heritage when we are young? Not many, I suppose. Youth is caught up in the immediacy of life; the past seems so irrelevant. Yet as we mature and experience the challenges and joys of life, we gain a new interest in our past. We begin to value the wealth of our heritage.

So it is with the way we view the great hymns of our faith. Some have grown up without a thought for the songs that helped carry the thread of Christianity down through the years. Others of us have sung the words over and over yet missed the truths to be found in the familiar melodies.

Hymns have been a part of my life since I was a child. These songs rang from the small church my father pastored in Oregon and resounded from the lips of saints in northern Argentina, where my parents later served as missionaries. During some of my growing-up years I mouthed the words in a lifeless routine, oblivious to their meaning. Later, I cast off the hymns for newer musical forms of expression.

In recent years I have come to appreciate the rich heritage of our great hymns. I have read the texts and studied their meaning. I have researched the hymn writers and sought to understand the circumstances that gave birth to their expressions of faith. As a result, I have caught glimpses of my Lord's majesty . . . power . . . tenderness . . . kindness . . . amazing grace. Along with newer forms of praise, these tested songs enrich my life and give voice to the deep stirrings of my heart.

God has spoken to us about himself and his son in other ways, of course. One of the ways God speaks to us is through nature. In the fragile unfolding of flower petals we can hear his powerfully creative words. In great vistas, in mountain heights and in sprawling fields of beauty we can hear of his unending majesty and greatness. All of it proclaims his sovereignty—and all of it points us to the Lord of all creation, the incomparable Lord Jesus Christ.

My prayer is that this volume will help you to look beyond the cares of this temporal world in which we live. That you will "hear" with inner ears the truths held so preciously in the words of our greatest hymns. That you will "see" with the eyes of faith the beautiful One. May the prayers that follow each meditation be the prelude to your own worship and adoration of our incomparable Lord Jesus Christ.

Your brother in Christ,

Steve Green

HOLY, HOLY, HOLY

Holy, holy, holy! Lord God Almighty!
Early in the morning
our song shall rise to Thee;
Holy, holy, holy! merciful and mighty!
God in three Persons, blessed Trinity!

Holy, holy, holy! all the saints adore Thee,
Casting down their golden crowns
around the glassy sea;
Cherubim and seraphim
falling down before Thee,
Which wert and art and evermore shalt be.

Holy, holy, holy!
though the darkness hide Thee,
Though the eye of sinful man
Thy glory may not see;
Only Thou art holy—
there is none beside Thee,
Perfect in power, in love and purity.

Holy, holy, holy! Lord God Almighty!
All Thy works shall praise Thy name
in earth and sky and sea;
Holy, holy, holy! merciful and mighty!
God in three Persons, blessed Trinity!

Jesus Christ is characterized as "holy, blameless, pure, set apart from sinners, exalted above the heavens" (Heb. 7:26). He never suffered a painful sense of separation from God because of a guilty conscience, as we do, because he never gave in to the pull of darkness or evil. Never once did he present the members of his body to sin, as instruments of wickedness; never did he mentally fight against his heavenly Father or resist his Father's will. And yet . . .

Jesus, our High Priest, can sympathize with us in all our weakness, because he was tempted in every way that we are. Only he was without sin. In his earthly life, he peered into the dark-shadowed deceit of the soul of mankind; and in his suffering on the cross, God laid upon Jesus' spotless soul the corruption of sin, the fearful darkness of death.

Because he was wholly faithful to God's will to the end, he became the perfect expression of all that is right and just and lovely. For us, he is the morning of our new, holy life in God.

—*Holy Christ, I praise you for your holiness before God.*
And I thank you that by joining myself to you
I can enjoy the priceless privilege of seeing God's holy
nature begin to dawn in me.

SPIRIT OF GOD,
DESCEND UPON MY HEART

Spirit of God, descend upon my heart:

Wean it from earth, through all its pulses move.

Stoop to my weakness, mighty as Thou art,

And make me love Thee as I ought to love.

Our children need us to instill in them a sense of confidence. We say, "You can do it. I know you can!" We praise them for achievement and ability. And we watch their spirits open to our voice. They need our words to encourage and train them. ❦ Yet in our relationship with God, there is a truth that must be acknowledged. We are powerless to please him—we are unable to right the wrongs we have done, and we cannot do what he asks of us. *We can't do it.* What a blow to our self-confidence. ❦ Jesus Christ says, "Apart from me you can do nothing" (John 15:5). We may be busy and boast a list of accomplishments to our credit—but it amounts to nothing before our God. ❦ *Christ alone fulfilled what we could not do.* He pleased the Father perfectly—in letter and in spirit—by living a sinless life. Only in him are we pleasing to God, justified from our sins. And only by his Spirit are we able to live a life that honors our heavenly Father.

❦

—Strong Lord, "stoop to my weakness, mighty as Thou art, and make me love Thee as I ought to love."

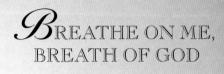REATHE ON ME, BREATH OF GOD

Breathe on me, Breath of God,
Fill me with life anew,
That I may love what Thou dost love,
And do what Thou wouldst do.

Breathe on me, Breath of God,
Till I am wholly Thine,
Until this earthly part of me
Glows with Thy fire divine.

Spirit—the Bible words for this aspect of God's being suggest wind or breath. In the beginning, God

formed man from the dust of the ground and breathed into his nostrils the breath of life. The

Scriptures say, "the breath of the Almighty gives me life" (Job 33:4). All life flows from our Creator.

❧ Then sin entered the world through Adam, and every person born in his lineage is born in sin. We

are sinners by birth and by choice. ❧ The Apostle Paul described our condition as *spiritually dead* and

separated from the life of God. Our greatest need, then, is spiritual life. God, who is rich in mercy,

because of his great love for us gives us new life in Jesus Christ. He breathes life into these mortal

bodies through his Spirit, who lives in every believer. Have you understood this gift from God?

—Jesus Christ, may I be fully alive to you,
for you are my very life—the breath of my soul.

SPIRIT OF THE LIVING GOD

Spirit of the Living God, fall fresh on me.

Spirit of the Living God, fall fresh on me.

Melt me, mold me, fill me, use me.

Spirit of the Living God,

fall fresh on me.

Dry spells are common to every believer—every man and woman of faith.

I remember facing a time of ministry and feeling quite lifeless. I did what I know to do: read my Bible, prayed. Yet there was little joy in it. I was aware that periods of dryness can be brought on by prolonged suffering, deep sorrow that has numbed our senses, or by a gradual drifting away from the Lord through neglect and compromise. A heart can become numb, and "fall asleep" to God. In my case, even though I could not think of anything that was specifically wrong, I knew that I was in need of refreshing from the Lord. Within a few days the Lord showed me an area of disobedience—a compromise I had made thinking it was not important. His mercy and forgiveness melted me. His strength empowered me to change. And then his joy restored my spirit.

What is your situation today? Are you in need of spiritual restoration? Would you be willing to pray with sincerity: "Melt me, mold me, fill me, use me"?

❧

—Living Lord, pour the water of your Spirit on the parched soil of my heart. Restore to me the joy of your salvation.

CHRIST THE LORD
IS RISEN TODAY

Christ the Lord is risen today,
Alleluia!
Sons of men and angels say:
Alleluia!
Raise your joys and triumphs high,
Alleluia!
Sing, ye heavens, and earth reply:
Alleluia!

Lives again our glorious King,
Alleluia!
Where, O death, is now thy sting?
Alleluia!
Dying once He all doth save,
Alleluia!
Where thy victory, O grave?
Alleluia!

Love's redeeming work is done,
Alleluia!
Fought the fight, the battle won,
Alleluia!
Death in vain forbids Him rise,
Alleluia!
Christ has opened Paradise,
Alleluia!

Soar we now where Christ has led,
Alleluia!
Following our exalted Head,
Alleluia!
Made like Him, like Him we rise,
Alleluia!
Ours the cross, the grave, the skies,
Alleluia!

JESUS

said, "I am the resurrection and the life" (John 11:25). He spoke these words in the face of a reality that haunts every human soul—death. Jesus arrived in Bethany purposefully late, knowing that his work there would be a lesson for all of his disciples through all time. Lazarus had been dead for four days. Those who loved Lazarus had trailed helplessly after him on the dark path—of sickness, frailty, death . . . following with tears, sorrow, grief.

Then Jesus came!

His words still give hope to our frail humanity: "He who believes in me will live, even though he dies; and whoever lives and believes in me will never die" (John 11:25).

—Risen Lord Jesus,
praise you for resurrection life now,
and eternal life to come.

The Lord's Prayer

Our Father, which art in heaven,

Hallowed be Thy name.

Thy kingdom come,

Thy will be done on earth as it is in heaven.

Give us this day our daily bread,

And forgive us our debts, as we forgive our debtors.

And lead us not into temptation but deliver us from evil;

For Thine is the kingdom, and the power, and the glory,

Forever, Amen.

During a prayer meeting, I was speaking out loud my agreement with the prayers of others. My son, Josiah, was beside me and at first I was unaware that his eyes were fixed on me. Then he began to copy my expressions and repeat what I was saying: "Yes, Lord. Praise you, Lord. Hallelujah!" Even though he was not involved in our praying, he was learning to pray.

There is so much that I do not understand about prayer. But I have chosen as my example and teacher, Jesus Christ. He lived a life of prayer, escaping frequently to talk to his Father. When the disciples asked for instruction, he taught them to pray. So often, when I want answers or knowledge or direction, I sense him saying to me, *pray*.

Not only does our Lord show us how to pray, but more wonderfully, he prays for us. He is our intercessor: ". . . he is able to save completely those who come to God through him, because he always lives to intercede for them" (Heb. 7:25). If God is for us, who can be against us? Our Lord is committed to the complete salvation of our souls. *Praise his name!*

—*Gracious Advocate, you are my Defender and Champion. I call out to you, knowing that you hear. Thank you for the treasure of communion through prayer.*

AND CAN IT BE?

And can it be that I should gain
An interest in the Savior's blood?
Died He for me, who caused His pain?
For me, who Him to death pursued?
Amazing love! how can it be
That Thou, my God, shouldst die for me?

Long my imprisoned spirit lay
Fast bound in sin and nature's night.
Thine eye diffused a quickening ray:
I woke—the dungeon flamed with light!
My chains fell off, my heart was free,
I rose, went forth, and followed Thee.

No condemnation now I dread:
Jesus, and all in Him, is mine!
Alive in Him, my living Head,
And clothed in righteousness divine,
Bold I approach the eternal throne,
And claim the crown, thru Christ my own.
Amazing love! how can it be
That Thou, my God, shouldst die for me!

Amazing love . . .

Every once in a while my calloused

heart receives a fresh breath of

Christ's love for me. Then I am

overtaken with wonder. All too

often I take for granted the gift of

salvation—a gift that even angels

view with awe.

I think it will not happen until I

enter eternity. Only then will I fully

comprehend the depths of God's

love. While I was guilty and

helpless, the spotless lamb of God

fully paid for my sins. Hallelujah,

what a Savior!

—Loving Lord Jesus, you have
opened my blind eyes. You have freed
me from captivity to sin. You have
released me from the dungeon of
darkness. From the depths of my
heart I praise you.

How
Great Thou Art

O Lord my God, when I in awesome wonder
Consider all the worlds Thy hands have made,
I see the stars, I hear the rolling thunder,
Thy power throughout the universe displayed.

Then sings my soul, my Savior God, to Thee:
How great Thou art, how great Thou art!
Then sings my soul, my Savior God to Thee:
How great Thou art, how great Thou art!

And when I think that God, His Son not sparing,
Sent Him to die, I scarce can take it in,
That on the cross, my burden gladly bearing,
He bled and died to take away my sin.

When Christ shall come with shout of acclamation
And take me home, what joy shall fill my heart!
Then I shall bow in humble adoration,
And there proclaim, my God, how great Thou art.

*A*few nights ago, my son and I went outside to lay on our backs and look up at the full moon and the stars. Have you done that lately?

Looking at the universe gives us a sense of perspective. The nearest star is our sun—and it is 93 million miles from earth. If the sun were hollow, it could contain 1½ million spheres the size of the earth. Light travels at 186,000 miles per second, and the next nearest star beyond the sun is 4½ light years away. There are approximately 100 billion stars in our galaxy, and with the most powerful telescope on earth scientists have discovered some 200 million other galaxies…. I lay there that evening feeling overwhelmed. Sir James Jeans, the British astronomer, stated that there are probably as many stars in the universe as there are grains of sand on every beach in the world. I can almost hear David whispering in awe, "Great is the Lord and most worthy of praise; his greatness no one can fathom" (Ps. 145:3).

—Creator and Lord, I am overwhelmed by your works and your omnipotence. I cannot comprehend your immensity. You hold all things together by your power. I rest in your greatness.

GREAT IS THY FAITHFULNESS

Great is Thy faithfulness, O God my Father,
There is no shadow of turning with Thee;
Thou changest not, Thy compassions they fail not;
As Thou hast been Thou forever will be.

Great is Thy faithfulness!
Great is Thy faithfulness!
Morning by morning new mercies I see;
All I have needed Thy hand hath provided—
Great is Thy faithfulness, Lord, unto me!

Pardon for sin and a peace that endureth,
Thine own dear presence to cheer and to guide;
Strength for today and bright hope for tomorrow,
Blessings all mine, with ten thousand beside!

A few nights ago, my son and I went outside to lay on our backs and look up at the full moon and the stars. Have you done that lately?

Looking at the universe gives us a sense of perspective. The nearest star is our sun—and it is 93 million miles from earth. If the sun were hollow, it could contain 1½ million spheres the size of the earth. Light travels at 186,000 miles per second, and the next nearest star beyond the sun is 4½ light years away. There are approximately 100 billion stars in our galaxy, and with the most powerful telescope on earth scientists have discovered some 200 million other galaxies.... I lay there that evening feeling overwhelmed. Sir James Jeans, the British astronomer, stated that there are probably as many stars in the universe as there are grains of sand on every beach in the world. I can almost hear David whispering in awe, "Great is the Lord and most worthy of praise; his greatness no one can fathom" (Ps. 145:3).

—Creator and Lord, I am overwhelmed by your works and your omnipotence. I cannot comprehend your immensity. You hold all things together by your power. I rest in your greatness.

GREAT IS THY FAITHFULNESS

Great is Thy faithfulness, O God my Father,
There is no shadow of turning with Thee;
Thou changest not, Thy compassions they fail not;
As Thou hast been Thou forever will be.

Great is Thy faithfulness!
Great is Thy faithfulness!
Morning by morning new mercies I see;
All I have needed Thy hand hath provided—
Great is Thy faithfulness, Lord, unto me!

Pardon for sin and a peace that endureth,
Thine own dear presence to cheer and to guide;
Strength for today and bright hope for tomorrow,
Blessings all mine, with ten thousand beside!

There is a plague of skepticism devouring our world. Who can we trust? Heroes fall; leaders mislead; friends forsake. Even the most sincere people fall short of their finest intentions. Where can we plant our feet and know we will not be let down?

Not long ago, I spoke with a woman who recently survived a dangerous earthquake. Having been through a quake myself, I could empathize with her fear and dismay. The one solid, dependable foundation—the earth—moves and ripples like water. Something deep inside you is hesitant to trust it again.

In the same way, the difficulties and calamities that are common to this life shatter our security and dishearten us. Doubt clouds our outlook.

Moses wrote, "He is the Rock, his works are perfect, and all his ways are just. A faithful God who does no wrong, upright and just is he" (Deut. 32:4). Here is a sure base on which we can fully depend. We can trust in the steadfastness of Jesus Christ, who is the same yesterday, today and forever!

—Faithful Lord, thank you for the certainty of your person, your word and your promises. By faith I plant my feet firmly on the rock of your unfailing love.

PRAISE TO THE LORD, THE ALMIGHTY

Praise to the Lord, the Almighty,
The King of creation!
O my soul, praise Him,
For He is thy health and salvation!
All ye who hear,
Now to His temple draw near;
Join me in glad adoration!

"Awake, my soul! Awake, harp and lyre! I will awaken the dawn" (Ps. 57:8).

A wake-up call usually starts my morning when I'm traveling. Time to get up; to rise and step into the work and the challenges and the joys of that twenty-four-hour slice of time. You and I need another wake-up call. One for the soul. We need to say with the psalmist, "Awake, my soul! I will awaken the dawn." We can choose to carelessly drift through the day—or to set our hearts on the Lord. We can waken our souls to the unceasing song of heaven: *"Worthy is the Lamb, who was slain, to receive power and wealth and wisdom and strength and honor and glory and praise!"* (Rev. 5:12).

Sometimes I feel lethargic; sometimes troubled or discouraged. Then I recall the psalm of David, which he sang to himself while hiding in a cave from vicious men who sought to kill him: "I will sing and make music. . . . I will praise you, O Lord . . . " (Ps. 57: 7, 9). Regardless of my circumstances, I am learning to draw near to God by lifting my soul through praise to the Lamb. And it's as if I am joining with a great company—the whole heavenly host—announcing the glory of the one who alone is worthy!

⚜

—Hallelujah. Along with everything that has breath,
I join in praise to you. My mouth will speak in praise to my God.
I will not be silent. Praise the Lord O my soul!

CROWN HIM WITH MANY CROWNS

Crown Him with many crowns,
The Lamb upon His throne:
Hark! how the heavenly anthem drowns
All music but its own!
Awake, my soul, and sing
Of Him who died for thee,
And hail Him as thy matchless King
Through all eternity.

The word *King* has little true significance to those of us who are not familiar with monarchy. Kings can either instill fear through tyrannical rule, or they are merely figureheads performing ceremonial duties. The prevailing attitude of today is reflected in a popular slogan—"question authority." We elect leaders to serve our best interests and would not tolerate absolute control. So often our leaders disappoint us.

How then do I respond to Jesus Christ as King? His kingdom is built upon righteousness. His throne is established with justice. He alone can demand full obedience, because all his ways are perfect and right. In this, he is matchless. Unlike the rulers of this earth who fail, Christ Jesus is *King Eternal, Immortal, Invisible,* the *Only God.*

—Glorious King, rule this servant.
May every thought, attitude and deed be done in
reverent submission to your holy will.

Jesus Shall Reign

Jesus shall reign wherever the sun

Does His successive journeys run;

His kingdom spread from shore to shore,

Till moons shall wax and wane no more.

Let every creature rise and bring

His grateful honors to our King;

Angels descend with songs again,

And earth repeat the loud "Amen!"

The psalmist often cried out at the inequities around him: the righteous suffered and the wicked seemed to prosper. But the Lord assures us that there is a "scroll of remembrance" being written—and some day we will see the distinction between those who serve the Lord and those who do not. The example of Christ himself was this: When he suffered, he entrusted himself to the wise Father who judges justly.

At present we do not see all things in subjection to God. Yet with full confidence we can rest in his supremacy, knowing that some day every wrong will be righted and every injustice fully recompensed—and all our faithfulness rewarded.

—Blessed Ruler,
till every knee bows before you,
I bow mine. Until the day every tongue
confesses you as Lord,
I will confess you to be Lord of all.
And Lord of this servant.

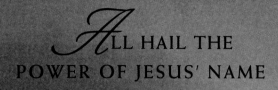

ALL HAIL THE POWER OF JESUS' NAME

All hail the power of Jesus' name!
Let angels prostrate fall;
Bring forth the royal diadem,
And crown Him Lord of all;
Bring forth the royal diadem,
And crown Him Lord of all!

Crown Him,
Crown Him,
Crown Him,
Crown Him,
And crown Him Lord of all.

WHAT'S IN A NAME? IN THE BIBLE, NAMES ARE NOT GIVEN MERELY FOR THE PURPOSE OF IDENTIFICATION. THEY EXPRESS THE VERY ESSENCE OF THE PERSON. NAMES WERE TIED TO PERSONALITY AND REPUTATION. JACOB MEANS "SUPPLANTER"—ONE WHO TAKES WHAT IS NOT HIS. NABAL MEANS "FOOL." ELIJAH MEANS "MY GOD IS YAHWEH." HOW IMPORTANT, THEN, MUST THE NAME "JESUS" BE.

JOSEPH AND MARY WERE GIVEN THE NAME JESUS BEFORE THE CHILD WAS BORN, BY GOD HIMSELF. IT IS USED OF OUR LORD SOME 939 TIMES IN THE NEW TESTAMENT. THE NAME JESUS EMBODIES ALL OF GOD'S HEART AND PURPOSE FOR US, FOR IT MEANS "SAVIOR." HE CAME TO SAVE US, HIS PEOPLE, FROM OUR SINS.

THERE IS NO MAGIC IN HIS NAME, NO SPECIAL CAPACITY FOR THOSE WHO UTTER IT. BUT WE ARE TOLD THAT "SALVATION IS FOUND IN NO ONE ELSE, FOR THERE IS NO OTHER NAME UNDER HEAVEN GIVEN TO MEN BY WHICH WE MUST BE SAVED" (ACTS 4:12).

ONLY JESUS, OUR MIGHTY SAVIOR, CAN FREE US FROM THE CLUTCHES OF SIN AND FROM THE DESTRUCTIVENESS OF SELF-CENTERED LIVING. ONLY HE CAN MAKE US ALIVE, WE WHO WERE DEAD IN TRANSGRESSIONS. AND ONLY HE CAN DEFEAT THE ENEMY OF OUR SOULS AND GRANT US EVERLASTING LIFE. ALL HAIL THE POWER OF JESUS' NAME!

*—Lord Jesus, I speak your name by faith and acknowledge you as my own Savior.
In you alone I find salvation and life. I know how utterly helpless I was to save myself and
so in deep gratitude I give praise to your holy name.*

FAIREST LORD JESUS

Beautiful Savior
Lord of all nature
O Thou of God and man the Son
Thee will I cherish
Thee will I honor
Thou my soul's glory, joy, and crown

Fair are the meadows
Fairer still the woodlands
Robed in the blooming garb of spring
Jesus is fairer
Jesus is purer
Who makes the woeful heart to sing

H ow

limited are our words as we try to describe the *beauty*

of Christ. The hymn writer wished for a "thousand

tongues" to sing his great Redeemer's praise. When I

most clearly see my Savior, when I catch a fresh glimpse

of his beauty, then I have no words to express his

splendor. I am taken into the wonder of silent worship.

In a feeble attempt I can speak of what is familiar to me

and compare my Lord to the glory of his creation—

or compare his love to the best love earth can offer.

Yet Jesus is infinitely fairer.

At last, I must acknowledge, paraphrasing the words

of the Apostle Peter, *Though I have not seen him I love him,*

and even though I do not see him now I believe in him and I am

filled with an inexpressible and glorious joy (1 Pet. 1:8).

—*Beautiful Lord Jesus, I long for the day when*
I can give voice for all eternity to the honor, glory and adoration
that you alone call forth in the silences of my soul!

OUR GREAT SAVIOR

Hallelujah! what a Savior!

Hallelujah! what a Friend!

Saving, helping, keeping, loving,

He is with me to the end.

Savior. I cherish this word, and consider it one of the most glorious titles given to our Lord Jesus.

Some only know the sweet baby Jesus of the manger in Bethlehem. Others are only acquainted with his teachings, as they are aware of other "philosophies." Some see him as a social hero—champion of the downtrodden, friend to prostitutes and tax collectors, comfort to the sick and destitute. Many see Christ's death on the cross, his meek submission to enemies. We can feel his compassion as we look into the searching eyes of the lost and hurting.

And yet it is possible to know all about this Christ, possible to embrace only certain aspects of his mission, and still not know him as *Savior*. His greatest work was this: to free us from our sins by his blood.

Jesus came to do for us what we could never do for ourselves. He ransomed us from Satan's kingdom; he rescued us from all darkness that would pursue us from behind; and he made a way for us to come before God, by pouring out his blood on the cross.

He is our only Savior!

—Lord and Savior, at just the right time, while I was powerless
to save myself, you saved me. Hallelujah!

MY JESUS, I LOVE THEE

My Jesus, I love Thee,
I know Thou art mine—
For Thee all the follies of sin I resign;
My gracious Redeemer,
My Savior art Thou:
If ever I loved Thee,
My Jesus, 'tis now.

How easily the word *love* is spoken—yet how often it becomes a dry husk of a word, with no life-giving power in it. I can tell everyone around me that I love them, but it means nothing unless I am demonstrating love in real and practical ways.

In song and in prayer I say that I love my Lord: And he says, "If you love me, you will obey what I command" (John 14:15).

Joyful obedience is the evidence of love. Let it be so . . . .

—My Jesus Christ, how can I not say that I love you?
Even through the frailties and inconsistencies of my life,
I confess that I have no other Savior and Master.
You alone are the One that I love.

Amazing Grace

Amazing grace! how sweet the sound—

That saved a wretch like me!

I once was lost but now am found,

Was blind but now I see.

When we've been there ten thousand years,

Bright shining as the sun,

We've no less days to sing God's praise

Than when we'd first begun.

My Jesus, I Love Thee

My Jesus, I love Thee,
I know Thou art mine—
For Thee all the follies of sin I resign;
My gracious Redeemer,
My Savior art Thou:
If ever I loved Thee,
My Jesus, 'tis now.

How easily the word *love* is spoken—yet how often it becomes a dry husk of a word, with no life-giving power in it. I can tell everyone around me that I love them, but it means nothing unless I am demonstrating love in real and practical ways.

In song and in prayer I say that I love my Lord: And he says, "If you love me, you will obey what I command" (John 14:15).

Joyful obedience is the evidence of love. Let it be so . . . .

—My Jesus Christ, how can I not say that I love you?
Even through the frailties and inconsistencies of my life,
I confess that I have no other Savior and Master.
You alone are the One that I love.

Amazing Grace

Amazing grace! how sweet the sound—

That saved a wretch like me!

I once was lost but now am found,

Was blind but now I see.

When we've been there ten thousand years,

Bright shining as the sun,

We've no less days to sing God's praise

Than when we'd first begun.

For many years I had a mistaken understanding about salvation. ❧ Yes, I acknowledged the fact that Jesus died for my sins and that I needed his saving. But my true thinking was still askew. I thought of myself as a relatively good person who needed a few improvements. My sin was not as bad as that of many others. I needed the death of Christ on the cross, but I supposed that it was a little easier for him to die for me than for some others. After all, I was a nice person, well groomed and educated. I was a good citizen and helped many people. It was not until I began to experience the destructiveness of my sin and to realize that my heart was filled with the same self-centered depravity as every other human being that a change took place. ❧ I saw my pride. ❧ On my knees one night, humbled by my failures, sick of my sin, I cried out to God for mercy. Amazing grace flowed from God's vast reservoir of love to this graceless heart. No words can express my gratitude.

—————✦—————

—Gracious Lord Jesus, when I had nothing to offer you, nothing to attract your love, you loved me and saved me. Hallelujah!